T0017777

LEVEL
1

Goats

Rose Davidson

NATIONAL
GEOGRAPHIC

Washington, D.C.

For Megan —R.D.

Published by National Geographic Partners, LLC, Washington, DC, 20036.

Designed by Yay! Design

The author and publisher gratefully acknowledge the expert content review of this book by Jason Detzel, senior livestock educator, Cornell Cooperative Extension, Cornell University, and the literacy review of this book by Mariam Jean Dreher, professor of reading education, University of Maryland, College Park.

Author's Note
This book discusses goats from some of the nine accepted species as well as some of the breeds within the domestic goat subspecies.

Photo Credits
Cover, Fuse/Getty Images; header (THROUGHOUT), tutsi/Shutterstock; vocab art (THROUGHOUT), Andrii Bezvershenko/Shutterstock; 1, Design Pics Inc/National Geographic Image Collection; 3, pirita/Shutterstock; 4-5, Medford Taylor/National Geographic Image Collection; 6, C. Slawik/Juniors/Alamy Stock Photo; 7 (UP), Linas T/Shutterstock; 7 (CTR), Design Pics Inc/National Geographic Image Collection; 7 (LO), Iakov Filimonov/Shutterstock; 8-9, Volga/Shutterstock; 10, Martin Willis/Minden Pictures; 11, Ten03/Shutterstock; 12 (UP), Louis Laurent Grandadam/Getty Images; 12 (LO), imass/Shutterstock; 13 (UP), Engin Sezer/Shutterstock; 13 (LO), EcoPrint/Shutterstock; 14-15, Helmut Corneli/Alamy Stock Photo; 16-17, Dudarev Mikhail/Shutterstock; 18 (UP), Nick Upton/Nature Picture Library; 18 (CTR), cynoclub/Shutterstock; 18 (LO), Aerostato/Shutterstock; 19 (UP), Greece/Alamy Stock Photo; 19 (CTR), Dudarev Mikhail/Shutterstock; 19 (LO), Maresa Pryor/National Geographic Image Collection; 20, schubbel/Shutterstock; 21, Yva Momatiuk and John Eastcott/Minden Pictures; 22-23, Dr. Axel Gebauer/Nature Picture Library; 24, Darrell Palmer-Swaine/Alamy Stock Photo; 25, Oscar Diez/Minden Pictures; 26, Konstantin Mikhailov/Nature Picture Library; 27, Matthieu Paley/National Geographic Image Collection; 28, Inga Spence/Alamy Stock Photo; 29, Paul Pound/Shutterstock; 30 (LE), Bolderay/Dreamstime; 30 (RT), nasidastudio/Shutterstock; 31 (UP LE), Shannon Hibberd; 31 (UP RT), blickwinkel/Wilken/Alamy Stock Photo; 31 (LO LE), irin-k/Shutterstock; 31 (LO RT), Coatesy/Shutterstock; 32 (UP LE), Klein & Hubert/Nature Picture Library; 32 (UP RT), Mike Mareen/Shutterstock; 32 (LO LE), Dr. Axel Gebauer/Nature Picture Library; 32 (LO RT), Sandra Leidholdt/Getty Images

Trade paperback ISBN:
978-1-4263-7537-8
Reinforced library binding ISBN:
978-1-4263-7552-1

Printed in the United States of America
23/WOR/1

Contents

Hello, Goats!

Let's get to know goats!

Goats are curious and smart.

They learn quickly and are full of
energy. They live together in groups.

All About Goats

Goats can be different sizes and colors. They can have long hair or short hair. Some have big, floppy ears. Others have smaller ears that stick up.

Grisons striped goats

Nubian goat

Saanen goat

markhor goat

Goats may look different.
But goats have many of
the same parts.

HORNS: Both male
and female goats
can have horns.

HAIR: Goat hair comes in
lots of lengths, patterns,
and colors. It can be brown,
black, tan, or white.

HOOVES: Thick hooves
help a goat walk on
rocky ground without
getting hurt.

EARS: Goat ears can be short or long. They can point up or droop down.

EYES: The centers of the eyes, called pupils, are shaped like rectangles. This helps goats see far away and far to each side.

WATTLES: Some goats have extra pieces of skin near their throats.

Wild Word

HOOVES: The hard covering on the feet of some animals

9

Where Goats Live

This wild goat has a thick coat and curved horns.

Some goats are wild. These goats can live in mountains, forests, and deserts. Their thick hair keeps them warm in cold weather.

Other goats live on farms. They help people. Wherever they live, goats stay together as a herd.

Wild Word

HERD: A group of animals that lives and eats together

Female goats make milk. On a farm,
people collect the milk.
They drink it or use
it to make cheese.

A farmer collects goat milk.

cheese made from goat milk

a blanket made
of goat hair

The hair of this Angora
goat is made into soft
yarn for knitting.

People also
use goat hair.
They make cozy
sweaters and blankets with it.

Finding Food

a goat herd in the Canary Islands in Spain

Goats don't stay in one place for meals. They move around on big patches of land. There, they graze in the fields.

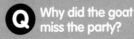

Wild Words

GRAZE: To eat grass that grows on the ground

BROWSE: To eat leaves, twigs, or other plant parts that grow up high

In the wild, they also find shrubs and other plants to browse. On a farm, they might be fed hay and grain, too.

15

Some goats help people just by eating. They eat plants that people don't want. They also eat dry plants that could catch fire. This helps keep wildfires from spreading.

Goats eat lots of weeds that people want to get rid of.

6 FUN FACTS About Goats

1
Some people keep **backyard goats** as **pets.**

2
Goat moms usually have **one to four babies** at a time— but **seven is the record!**

3
In Morocco, **goats climb trees** to eat **fruit** on the branches.

4 Male goats with horns use them **to fight.**

5 A female goat is called a **doe** or a **nanny.** A male goat is called a **buck** or a **billy.**

6 The Boer (BORE) goat is **one of the biggest goats.** It can weight up to **250 pounds.**

Growing Up

Baby goats, called kids, are born in the spring. A kid can stand up just a few minutes after it is born! Kids stay close to their mother. The mother goat makes milk for the kids to drink.

a young kid

older kids with their mother in the Pyrenees (PEER-uh-neez) mountains in France

As the kids get older, they stay with their mother's herd.

Adult goats with their young find plenty of food in their mountain home.

The kids start to eat plants. They look for food with the other goats.

On the Move

Goats are good jumpers. They jump over streams. They jump to get from one rock to another. Young goats also jump when they play.

Goat kids like to run and jump together.

An ibex (EYE-beks) goat in Spain easily jumps from one rock face to the next.

A tur goat climbs on a rock face.

Goats are good climbers, too. They can stay on their feet on rocky mountain cliffs. They can even climb on people!

Have you heard of goat yoga? In this yoga class, small goats climb on people's backs.

Good Night, Goats!

During the day, goats may rest or nap. At night, it's time to sleep.

Sometimes people put clothes on goats to keep them warm.

They snuggle together until the morning comes. Then they start a new day.

What in the World?

These pictures are up-close views of things in a goat's world. Use the hints to figure out what's in the pictures. Answers are on page 31.

1

HINT: This is a group of goats that lives together.

2

HINT: Goats jump from one of these to another.

horns	grass	herd	kid	hair	rock

3

HINT: Some male goats use these to fight.

4

HINT: This is a baby goat.

5

HINT: Goats eat lots of this plant.

6

HINT: This keeps a goat warm.

Answers: 1. herd, 2. rock, 3. horns, 4. kid, 5. grass, 6. hair

BROWSE: To eat leaves, twigs, or other plant parts that grow up high

GRAZE: To eat grass that grows on the ground

HERD: A group of animals that lives and eats together

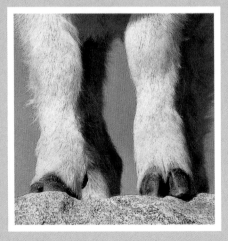

HOOVES: The hard covering on the feet of some animals